A POCKET GUIDE TO PARISH AFFAIRS

Also published by Mowbray

A POCKET GUIDE TO THE ANGLICAN CHURCH by Ronald H. Lloyd

A POCKET DICTIONARY OF THE CHRISTIAN CHURCH by Arthur L. Moore

A POCKET CALENDAR OF SAINTS AND PEOPLE TO REMEMBER
by Brother Kenneth, CGA

A POCKET GUIDE FOR SERVERS
by Raymond Wilkinson

A POCKET GUIDE TO CHRISTIAN BELIEF by Jean Smith

A POCKET GUIDE TO THE LIFE AND MEANING OF JESUS by Arthur L. Moore

A POCKET GUIDE TO WALSINGHAM
by Charles Smith

A Pocket Guide to Parish Affairs

Organisation and Administration in the Church of England

by

PETER E. HATTERSLEY

FOREWORD BY
THE RT REVD DAVID MICHAEL HOPE
Bishop of Wakefield

MOWBRAY
LONDON & OXFORD

ISBN 0-264-67166-X

First published 1988
by A. R. Mowbray & Co. Ltd,
Saint Thomas House, Becket Street,
Oxford, OX1 1SJ

Typeset and Printed by
David Green Printers Ltd, Kettering

British Library Cataloguing in Publication Data

Hattersley, Peter E.
A pocket guide to parish affairs.
1. Church of England
283'.42

ISBN 0-264-67166-X

FOREWORD

I am delighted to write a few words at the beginning of this useful and interesting publication. It clearly is needed as a means to try and explain some of the frequently used yet often misunderstood words and phrases in the Church of England. I hope that it will reach the folk in the churches who perhaps feel bamboozled by jargon. I commend the work and I am certain it will prove to be an invaluable addition to most church bookstalls.

+ *David Wakefield*

CONTENTS

PREFACE

This guide is intended to offer background information about the Church of England in an easily accessible form.

To avoid the repetition of important information the reader is invited to make cross-reference to sections of the text indicated, where key words are printed in *italics*.

Where further information is required, reference is suggested to publications listed in the bibliography at the end of this booklet.

P E H

Annual Parish Meeting

This meeting must be held not later than 30 April.

Notices announcing this meeting and the Annual Vestry Meeting must be posted on or near the church door at least two Sundays before the appointed date. For centuries, the Annual Vestry Meeting attended by all adult residents in the parish elected the *Churchwardens* but it is now customary for this meeting to be held immediately before the Annual Parish Meeting which may be attended by any person on the *Electoral Roll* of the parish, in effect members of the church aged sixteen years or upwards. The Vestry Meeting elects the Churchwardens; the Annual Meeting elects *Parochial Church Councillors* and members of the *Deanery Synod,* and appoints Sidesmen and Sideswomen: the Treasurer appointed by and from the PCC presents the audited accounts of the parish and makes a report of the finances of the parish which are controlled by the PCC (other financial arrangements are the responsibility of the Diocesan Finance Committee). It is customary for the *incumbent* and the PCC Secretary to give reports of their activities during the year and for representatives of various organizations to describe their activities. The chair is taken by the *incumbent, vicar* or *rector,* and members have the opportunity to ask questions and share in discussions or to introduce items for consideration having given notice to the Secretary prior to the meeting.

The Auditor of the church accounts, if not appointed

at the Annual Meeting, is appointed by the PCC and the financial statement to the AGM is first approved by the PCC; it is usual to circulate copies of the audited accounts at the AGM.

* * *

Archdeacon

In medieval times a bishop was assisted by lowly deacons, one of whom would travel with him and thus have opportunities to influence him. By the early thirteenth century, the office of senior deacon had emerged and he had to be present at the meetings of local clergy where his relationship with the bishop led to his office superseding that of the archpriest who presided at the chapter. The office of archpriest *(rural dean)* became moribund but was revived in 1836.

Archdeacons, usually two in number, are priests of at least six years seniority appointed by a diocesan *bishop* as Bishop's Officers to assist him in the management of the affairs of his diocese. They have territorial responsibility especially for the maintenance of church buildings and properties. By law they are the protectors of much of England's architectural heritage: all churches must be inspected every five years by an architect at the expense of the *PCC* and churchwardens must account for the buildings at the Archdeacon's *visitation*. Archdeacons issue certificates to approve minor repairs and redecoration. They also advise on *faculties*.

Archdeacons were, and not unkindly are, The Bishop's Eye with the duty of keeping him informed and alerting him to the needs of the Archdeaconry dispensing praise as well as blame. Archdeacons have a pastoral role with clergy and their families: although ordinands are usually examined by especially appointed chaplains the archdeacon normally presents candidates at Ordination Services.

The Archdeacon *inducts* a clergyman to his benefice – that is, he confirms an incumbent, after *institution*, in the possessions of the living. As members of the senior hierarchy of the diocese, archdeacons chair committees and working parties on behalf of the bishop; the senior of them is a member of the House of Clergy at the General *Synod*. In some dioceses the role of archdeacon is held by a suffragan bishop.
Archdeacons have the prefix 'The Venerable Archdeacon of . . .' and are styled 'The Venerable . . .X . . .Y'.

Banns of Marriage

These are notices of intention to be married, published at the parish church of the bride and bridegroom, during a Morning or Evening Service, on three dates within twelve weeks of the proposed wedding; they are a legal requirement within the Church of England, giving anyone who has just cause to inform the parish priest of any impediment to the legal marriage of the two named persons. Subject to there being no declared impediment and the presentation of Certificates of Banns, the marriage service can then take place. The solemnization of a marriage by a duly appointed clergyman of the Church of England, being the Established Church, has full legality; the civil registrar is not involved (refer *marriage*).

Baptism

Baptism is the sacrament instituted by Christ for those who wish to become members of His Church. It is normal for the vicar to meet with the parents of children seeking baptism for their child or with adults who wish to be baptized to explain the significance of baptism and the procedure of the service. Usually baptism is administered within another service when the congregation is larger than the child's/adult's immediate family, e.g. Mattins, Evensong or Holy Communion which emphasizes that the person has been admitted into the Church of Christ. The membership will be confirmed when the person chooses to renew his/her Baptismal vows at the Service of *Confirmation* conducted by a bishop.

Baptism services can be conducted by any ordained deacon or priest and by deaconesses. At the baptism of children, presented by their parents, each has at least three Godparents who take vows on their behalf and promise to give them the help and encouragement they need.

* * *

Bishop

Bishop is the most senior in the order of clergy – bishop, priest, deacon.

Historically, bishops were given 'ordinary' jurisdiction in ecclesiastical matters within their dioceses. They take an oath of obedience to the archbishop of their province; other clergy take oaths of obedience to them: bishops exercise original as distinct from delegated jurisdiction. In ruling his diocese the bishop must conform to secular law as far as it is applicable to his actions.

Diocesan bishops are appointed by the Sovereign, as Head of the Church of England, on the advice of the Prime Minister, because the Church of England is the

Established Church. When seeking diocesan bishops, the Patronage Secretary, a Crown appointment, takes opinions from whomsoever he wishes, including persons who have knowledge of the diocese; twelve members of the Crown Appointments Commission of the General Synod (the 2 archbishops, 4 diocesan Bishops, 3 House of Laity, 3 House of Clergy) present two names in alphabetical order unless there is a two-thirds majority in favour of one of them, then this is indicated; the Prime Minister then submits one of the names to the Sovereign.

By ancient custom this person is then formally elected by the *Chapter* of the *Cathedral* and if not already a bishop, is consecrated with due ceremony by the Archbishop; bishops who are appointed diocesan bishops are enthroned in their cathedral by the *Dean/Provost*.

One or more suffragan bishops may be appointed to assist diocesan bishops in pastoral care. Clergy who have served as bishops overseas often return to England and assist diocesan bishops. Bishops are paid from funds managed by the *Church Commissioners*. Bishops are styled 'The Right Reverend X. . . Y. . .'. The Archbishop of Canterbury signs 'Robert Cantuar', the Bishop of Wakefield, 'David Wakefield', the Bishop of Durham, 'David Dunelm'.

The bishop of the diocese is charged with the spiritual leadership of his territory and has responsibility for the conduct of the clergy. He has no responsibility for the activities of individual parishes nor for the activities of individual clergymen except of those whom he licenses to officiate within his diocese. He approves the appointment of beneficed clergy to their *parishes*. He ordains priests and deacons, shares in the consecration of other bishops, holds institutions, conducts confirmation services and fulfils every other duty of a priest. He presides over the Diocesan *Synod,* and its several committees; he is a member of the House of Bishops of the General Synod, and if of sufficient seniority, a member of the House of Lords. He is advised by various groups of clergy and lay people, including The Bishop's Council, and can appoint clergy of distinction as Honorary Canons in his Cathedral whose day to day affairs are in the hands of the *Dean/Provost*.

Since 1847, twenty-six bishops sit in the House of Lords; Canterbury, York, London, Durham and Winchester and twenty-one in order of seniority as diocesan bishops. The most senior bishop is the Archbishop of Canterbury, styled 'The Most Reverend', Primate of all England; the Archbishop of York, Primate of England, is responsible for the Northern Province (fourteen dioceses). Bishops once appointed retire at will although those appointed since 1976 will retire aged seventy.

An archbishop as Metropolitan has the supervision of the bishops in his province without having legal authority over any: he must act with them as individuals: nevertheless, he exercises significant influence (refer *establishment*). The Archbishop of

Canterbury crowns the monarch, can bestow academic degrees and issue licences throughout both provinces by powers acquired as Primate of all England at the Reformation.

Buildings

The churches and their associated buildings, other than the parsonage houses (vicarages) are in the care of the *Parochial Church Council.* The cost of their maintenance falls on the parish but the standard is determined by the Diocesan Advisory Committee and the appropriate *archdeacon.* Financial aid may be obtained from the *Church Commissioners* under certain circumstances.

Canon Law

Canon Law or Church Law is the compendium of Statutes or Acts of Parliament, Orders in Council, Measures of the Church Assembly and, since 1969, of Canons determined by the General Synod which affect the Church of England as the Established Church and regulate the life of the Church. All functions of the Church of England are based upon it. The Church Assembly, created in 1919, was replaced in 1969 by the General Synod, which can pass measures, having the effect of statutes. The General Synod must approve by two-thirds majority any Canon or regulation which establishes a general rule of priniciple or practice for the Church of England.

Canon

Canons are priests who are members of the Cathedral *Chapter*. Residentiary canons work full-time at the Cathedral; other clergy are appointed as honorary canons by the bishop in recognition of personal qualities or service: canons are allocated a stall or seat in the Cathedral and as the Cathedral Chapter elect an incoming bishop. With their informal seniority in the diocese they take a prominent part in its affairs.

Cathedral

The church in which the Bishop has his seat ('cathedral') irrespective of its location, age, size or architectural distinction.

Cathedrals of the 'Old' Foundation e.g. Exeter, Lincoln, London (St Paul's), Salisbury, York date from before the Reformation; after the Dissolution of the Monasteries by Henry VIII some abbeys became 'New' Cathedrals, e.g. Durham, Norwich, Winchester, Canterbury and five other cathedrals were created, Oxford, Chester, Bristol, Gloucester and Peterborough. No new dioceses were then created until Ripon in 1836.

With the growth and shift of population in the nineteenth century, seven new dioceses were formed, e.g. Manchester (1847); St Albans (1877); Liverpool (1880); Wakefield (1888): twelve since 1900, e.g. Birmingham (1905); Sheffield (1914); St Edmundsbury and Ipswich (1914); Bradford (1919); Portsmouth (1927). Sixteen existing parish churches were raised to Cathedral Status and are known as 'Modern' cathedrals; Truro, Liverpool, Coventry and Guildford are newly built.

Each cathedral is governed by its Dean and Chapter if of ancient foundation and by its Provost and Chapter if more recent or a 'parish church' cathedral. The Crown appoints the dean in the Old and New [illegible]drals and the Diocesan Bishop appoints the

In respect of its own activities the cathedral has a Cathedral Council, or, if also a parish church, its own Parochial Church Council and its parish clergy, although its senior clergy are usually canons and members of the chapter.

A newly appointed bishop is enthroned in the cathedral by the Dean/Provost.

The cathedral is frequently the venue for ceremonial occasions of interest to the whole diocese or to the community at large. Many cathedrals are buildings of the highest architectural distinction which it is the obligation of the Church to preserve.

Chancellor

The highest legal officer in a diocese, a barrister of at least seven years standing. He is judge of the Consistory Court which issues *Faculties:* he sits with two lay and two clerical assessors when the court deals with certain disciplinary proceedings involving the clergy arising from allegations of misconduct or neglect of duty. All common licences for marriage are issued in the name of the Chancellor; he also has legal responsibilities associated with the enthronement of a bishop and the installation of a Dean or Provost.

Chapter

The governing body of a Cathedral under the leadership of the *Dean* or *Provost*. Residentiary canons and honorary canons are charged with the administration of the Cathedral and, for the diocese, with the election of the bishop and consequent ceremonials. Other clergy work in the Cathedral which, if it is a parish church, also has its own *Parochial Church Council*.

Church Commissioners

These are appointed by statute to have control of the finances of the Church of England all of which originate from private legacies, endowments and gifts, not public funds. The Commissioners are the successors of the administrators of Queen Anne's Bounty (1704) and the Ecclesiastical Commissioners

(1836) and were set up in 1948 to manage the 'Historic Endowments' of the Church of England.

Queen Anne had restored all revenues previously paid as taxes to the Crown by the clergy from the income of their benefices so as to provide funds for the equitable distribution of resources to the clergy (and parishes) at large. In 1836 the incomes of Bishops were re-apportioned to correct glaring inequalities and to augment the poor livings of clergy, who were still generally dependent on the level of Patronage. These were major problems in unendowed parishes which had been created to meet the needs of the rapidly expanding population in developing industrial areas.

There are 95 Commissioners; 2 Archbishops, 41 Diocesan Bishops, 5 Deans/Provosts; 10 clergy and 10 Laity appointed by the General Synod; 4 lay persons appointed each by the Crown and by the Archbishop of Canterbury; 10 Officers of State, 3 representatives of the city of London, a representative of the city of York and 2 representatives of the universities of Oxford and Cambridge plus 3 Estates Commissioners. They meet annually but the Board of Governors (30) to whom the three Estates Commissioners report, meet almost monthly – the Archbishops of Canterbury and York; 6 diocesan bishops; 10 clergy and 7 laity appointed by General Synod, 2 of the Commissioners nominated by the Archbishop of Canterbury and the 3 Estates Commissioners.

The first Estates Commissioner is appointed by the

Crown, the third by the Archbishop of Canterbury; both are effectively full time and salaried. The second Estates Commissioner is a Member of Parliament who presents the affairs of the Church of England to the House of Commons, including the presentation of the Measures of the General *Synod.*

The Commissioners manage the historical assets of the church – land, property, and the stocks and shares portfolio whether acquired from ancient bequests or recent donations. From the income derived from these sources and direct giving, they are responsible for maintaining church buildings and supporting the clergy in the widest sense.

Acting as the Central Stipend Authority they arrange the stipends of the clergy in negotiation with the dioceses, give grants to non-beneficed clergy, e.g. university, polytechnic and Church of England College Chaplains; they provide housing for clergy, pensions for clergy and their widows and can arrange mortgages for retired clergy.

As the body responsible for pastoral reorganization since 1983 and for the disposal of redundant churches, they organize the sale and re-use of church properties and absorb the yields into their central funds.

They receive voluntary offerings via dioceses from parishes so that the total income and expenditure of the Church of England comes within their terms of reference. Their resources also finance training for the Ministry and lay workers; Missions; administration of diocese and parishes.

The only state money involved in the support of the Church of England is in salaries paid to Church of England Chaplains in prisons, hospitals and the armed services.

About half the income of the Church Commissioners is spent on the Ministry, about £150 million annually in the ratio 30% stipends, 8% housing, 10% pensions, 1% training.

The remainder of its income is spent in the ratio: 19% buildings, 12% public worship, 9% organization expenses, 5% parish expenses and 6% to education and missions.

Of its income in the order of £350 million, 42% comes from investments of all kinds – land, property, shares; 54% from voluntary giving and 4% from parochial and clergy fees. Thus 42% of the costs of 'running the Church of England' is not met directly by its members. None of the income of the Church of England comes from public funds.

Both income and expenditure fluctuate from year to year and inflation plays its part. The Church of England, as a recognized charity enjoys charitable status which brings some exemption from certain taxation and enables it to benefit from deeds of covenant. The Commissioners encourage all those who give, in whatever way, short of a legacy, to 'covenant their giving' and so obtain relief on the rate of basic tax, e.g. when income tax is 27% every £1 covenanted brings £1.37 to church funds.

* * *

Churchwardens

Churchwardens were historically the elected officers of the parish charged with responsibility for the buildings and property of the parish and the worship at the parish church. Churchwardens, who must normally be communicant members of the Church of England and over twenty-one years of age, are elected at a joint meeting of persons whose names are entered on the church electoral roll, and those who reside in the parish and are local government electors. This meeting is usually held immediately before the *Annual Parish Meeting*. The churchwardens must keep an inventory of buildings; all the furniture and chattels of the church premises are vested in the churchwardens but the incumbent has custody of the keys. The care, maintenance, preservation and insurance of the fabric and the contents are nowadays the responsibility of the PCC.

Churchwardens must maintain order during church services, and are responsible for the collection of alms and other monies disposed of by the PCC. Churchwardens must attend the archdeacon's visitation before assuming office; they are officers of the bishop and have a duty to keep him informed of the affairs and needs of their parish – especially important if 'things are going wrong'.

It is customary for one of the wardens to act as elected vice-chairman of the PCC.

* * *

Communion

Holy Communion or Eucharist is the colloquial name for the Order of the Administration of the Lord's Supper; it is the most significant sacrament of the Christian Church; the service, whose form has in essence changed little over the centuries, must be presided over by a priest who will distribute consecrated bread and wine to all participants who have been *'confirmed';* it is customary for children and other members of thc congregation to receive a blessing at the altar rail as an alternative. The president may be assisted by other clergy or especially commissioned lay people in the distribution of the sacraments. It is common for churches to arrange a Family Service including Eucharist or Parish Communion with sermon and music as the main service on Sundays. Holy Communion is often said or sung during the week as well as on Sundays.

* * *

Confirmation

This service combines the renewal of baptismal vows with the laying on of hands so that those who renew the promises made in their name at baptism assume full membership of the Church. Candidates are usually no younger than thirteen and are normally prepared by the parish clergy over several weeks prior to the service at which only a bishop, by laying on of hands, confirms. Those now confirmed can receive Holy Communion, usually later on the same occasion.

Deacon

Deacon is the most junior order of the clergy, for which women also became eligible in March 1987. Being over twenty-two and having satisfied the bishop of a diocese of their suitability for preparation for ordination, ordinands follow a course of theological training which may be full-time or part-time. When their initial training is completed ordinands are ordained deacon by a diocesan bishop or another bishop acting for him and normally serve in a parish within his diocese under the guidance of an experienced priest, normally the incumbent of that parish. Deacons are styled 'The Reverend . . .X . . .Y'.

Around 300 men and women are trained annually for the diaconate and in an attempt to distribute clergy evenly amongst the dioceses are allocated by a quota scheme and placed so as to further their training rather than to relieve the burdens of parochial clergy. Deacons are paid by the diocese and are provided with housing; they receive expenses of office from the PCC.

A deacon may conduct Mattins and Evensong (omitting the Absolution and Blessing), share but not preside at Holy Communion and conduct baptisms and funerals. A male deacon usually seeks ordination as a priest after one year's service but continues to serve in a parish for a further period as a priest before seeking his own 'living'. At his ordination as a priest fellow priests share with the bishop the laying on of hands.

Similarly those who are Non-Stipendiary Ministers are ordained as deacons and work in a parish which need not be their 'home' parish.

The training of clergy is expensive and is paid for via parish and diocesan quotas by the Church Commissioners and is supervised by the Advisory Council for the Church's Ministry. All clergy are expected to follow a period of Post-Ordination Training.

Deaconess

Dioceses are also able to appoint a number of (paid) deaconesses to work in parishes, who after a ceremony of laying on of hands may take Morning and Evening Prayer (omitting the Absolution and Blessing), distribute the sacrament, read lessons, preach, baptize, officiate at funerals and publish banns. All deaconesses are aged over twenty-five and swear an oath of obedience to the bishop in whose diocese they are licensed to work. Nevertheless, they remain members of the laity.

Dean

The Dean is the head of the *Chapter* and thus the senior amongst the cathedral clergy. He is effectively in charge of the clerical and lay staff at the cathedral. His equivalent in a 'parish church' cathedral is known as the *Provost*.

As the responsibilities of a bishop increased in medieval times the control of worship and administration in his cathedral passed into the hands of the Dean and Chapter (e.g. Precentor, Chancellor, Treasurer) who became virtually independent of the bishop.

As a senior member of the diocesan clergy he will take a prominent role in its affairs generally. Deans are styled 'The Very Reverend, the Dean . . .X . . .Y.'

Diocese

A diocese is the territorial area in the care of the bishop. There are forty-three dioceses in England, including Sodor and Man, each divided into two or more archdeaconries, themselves sub-divided into rural *deaneries,* in order to facilitate adminstration. Each diocese is under the jurisdiction of a *bishop* who will be assisted by one or more suffragan bishops. At his consecration, the bishop has taken an oath of obedience to the Archbishop of his province and on his enthronement he commits himself to the service of the diocese. Each diocese has a *Chancellor, Registrar,* Diocesan Secretary and other administrative officers to service various directorates, e.g. Finance, Education, Social responsibility, normally based in the Cathedral city. Each diocese has a Diocesan Synod elected from the Deanery Synod, with a House of Clergy and a House of Laity, and a Bishop's Council to advise and assist the bishop. There is also a Bishop of the diocese in Europe with responsibility for the Anglican Church in Europe.

* * *

Electoral Roll

An Electoral Roll Officer must be appointed by the PCC to maintain the roll. Any baptized person aged sixteen or over resident within a parish boundary or for six months an habitual attender at public worship at the parish church may enrol. Any communicant aged seventeen years or over may be elected to the PCC; those aged eighteen may be elected to the Deanery Synod; those aged twenty-one, and being a communicant, may be elected a churchwarden. Anyone aged sixteen may become a Sidesman or Sideswoman. The roll must be revised every six years.

* * *

Establishment

Her Majesty the Queen is Head of the Church of England – the sovereign of the United Kingdom must be a member of the Church of England. Because it is the Established Church, the legal basis of the affairs of the Church of England, including its orders of worship, is governed by Acts of Parliament – the authority of the General Synod is determined by the Church of England Assembly (Powers) Act 1919 as amended in 1969 – its Measures have the same force and effect as Acts of Parliament (the Second Church Estates Commissioner, who is unpaid, is a Member of Parliament who presents the Measures to the House of Commons).

The Archbishop of Canterbury takes precedence immediately after the royal princes: the Archbishop of York takes precedence after the Lord Chancellor (the highest officer of state), and above all but royal dukes.

The Archbishops of Canterbury and York, the Bishops of London, Durham and Winchester plus twenty-one other English diocesan bishops in order of seniority as diocesans, sit in the House of Lords during their episcopacy; these bishops may not vote in General Elections and no Church of England clergyman may offer himself as a Parliamentary Candidate; no Church of England clergyman may serve on a jury.

Establishment brings recognition of Church Courts as possessing legal jurisdiction. Only Anglicans may be appointed to certain professorships at Oxford, Cambridge and Durham universities and as Chaplain to the Speaker of the House of Commons. Establishment also enables a priest of the Church of England to conduct a marriage service in his own right without the involvement of a Registrar of Marriages.

An Act of Parliament could and still can affect any alteration whatsoever in the law of the Church.

The State or Government contributes nothing towards the expenses of the Church of England.

Faculties

These are very important legal documents issued by the Chancellor of a diocese usually on the application of the incumbent and churchwardens. Faculties authorize proposed changes in the fabric or furnishing of a church or its associated buildings. In the case of minor work an Archdeacon's certificate may be issued instead of a faculty. Stated requirements have to be met and appropriate fees paid. The Church of England is exempt from severe restrictions imposed on 'listed' buildings by a privilege known as the Ecclesiastical Exemption and the Faculty Jurisdiction is the means used to regulate alterations to church buildings of historic importance. Along with other recognized bodies, the Church of England can receive upkeep grants from public funds for the maintenance of historic churches. The Archdeacon is entitled to intervene in cases in which faculties are sought. The persons applying for a faculty are known as petitioners and are usually responsible for paying the fees and costs.

Festivals

Festivals are special days in the calendar of the Church when Christians are expected to take Holy

Communion – Christmas, Easter, Ascension, Whitsun.

The altar, pulpit and lectern in churches are often dressed during services in colours corresponding to the vestments, if any, worn by the president at the Holy Communion Service. Different colours are associated with different times in the Church's year but on Christmas Day and Easter Sunday it is usual to use the most precious embroideries available. The appropriate colours are:

Advent	– purple
Christmastide	– white
Eastertide	– white
Whitsunday	– red
Trinity Sunday	– white
Sundays after Pentecost	– green
Saints' Days	– white
Martyred Saints' Days	– red

Altars, pulpits and lecterns are stripped from the Evening of Maundy Thursday until Easter Eve.

* * *

Finance

The Church of England has both national and local sources of income and national and local financial obligations. Broadly, these relate to the costs of providing and maintaining the clerical and lay ministry, the costs of providing and maintaining churches and other church properties and the costs of worship and allied activities including training and missions.

The *Church Commissioners* handle the capital assets and income and distribute their proceeds among the clergy through the several dioceses as stipends, housing and pensions and meet the administrative costs of the church etc. Parish clergy are paid an annual salary within the current diocesan scale, as agreed with the Commissioners; each incumbent is provided with a house (vicarage) in which he is obliged to live during the period of his incumbency.

The income of a clergyman is his stipend (national minimum, April 1987, £8000), his house and his non-contributory pension scheme (full pension £4930 from April 1987). Parish clergy pass fees received for weddings and funerals whether at their church or at a Crematorium, and net income from chaplaincies into the diocesan 'pool'. They must live in 'tied' accommodation. Parishes normally pay their expenses of office.

Accommodation is also provided for full time curates according to need, but no housing aid is available to non-stipendiary ministers (refer *deacons*).

Over the centuries well wishers, especially during the nineteenth century, left land or made other endowments for the benefit of particular parishes but during the last fifty years massive equalization arrangements have been agreed and whilst dioceses still have different minima the wide differentials between the incomes of beneficed clergy (incumbents) once common have virtually disappeared.

PAROCHIAL FINANCE

The *PCC* receives its income from the weekly giving of its parishioners, from the profits of fund raising efforts and casual donations. The PCC has an obligation to pay its share towards the cost of administering the *diocese* and must meet the costs of maintaining, heating, lighting and cleaning the church and other buildings, the expenses of the services, the approved expenses of office of its clergy; discretionary payments to charities and organizations: the maintenance of the graveyard, for which it can levy fees. The QUOTA – a very heavy charge on most parishes is agreed at the Deanery *Synod* and is calculated by complicated formulae determined individually by dioceses which, for example, may take into account the total attendance on four nominated services in a month, say in May – the total of Easter and Christmas communicants – the size and sort of membership, i.e. the social mix; the population of the parish; trust income: a factor is thus discovered which determines the proportion of the diocesan costs to be paid by the individual parish.

* * *

Funerals

Priests, deacons, deaconesses and readers may conduct a funeral service on request either in their own or another licensed church, chapel or crematorium. Arrangements for burial in churchyards of a parish church are made with the vicar. There is a statutory scale of fees, locally applied. In the case of a cremation, the service may precede or follow the committal.

* * *

Graveyard (Churchyard)

Any land belonging to a church available for burials is the sole responsibility of the incumbent and PCC; this includes the maintenance of ground, the provision and maintenance of walls and the arrangements of burials entirely from their own financial resources (refer *archdeacon*). Burials are arranged at the discretion of the incumbent who may also approve the placing of memorials in the churchyard. The PCC levies discretionary fees for interments. In many boroughs, municipal cemeteries are provided and are maintained by the local authority which levies its own fees. The maintenance of an unused graveyard formally closed by Order in Council becomes after transfer from the PCC the responsibility of the Local

Authority. A local authority can undertake maintenance of other closed or disused graveyards by financial arrangement with the PCC.

* * *

Holy Orders

There are three holy orders, deacon, priest and bishop, in ascending order; the bishops are responsible for ordaining men and women to the diaconate and deacons to the priesthood; an archbishop supported by other bishops consecrates priests to the episcopacy. Some clerks in holy orders carry titles relating to their specific functions or duties. e.g. deans, provosts; archdeacons, rural deans; prebendaries, canons; rectors, vicars, curates; chaplains, precentors, assistant or suffragan bishops; archbishops. All ordained clergy use the title 'The Reverend'.

* * *

Incumbent

The incumbent is the clergyman given title to a living, in charge of a parish, colloquially called Vicar, or

Rector in some ancient parishes which had glebe attachments. His responsibilities are laid down in church law but he shares many of them with the *PCC*. After his Institution by the *bishop* he is inducted by the *archdeacon* and thereafter assumes full spiritual and temporal responsibilities. He can resign his living at will whilst still remaining a priest, but if appointed after 1976 must retire at age seventy although if the PCC consents the bishop may extend his service for up to two years. The widow of an incumbent may reside in the vicarage for two months.

Induction

After the *institution* of a newly appointed incumbent by the Bishop which gives him charge of the 'care of souls' of which notice was given at least one month earlier, the priest is Inducted, in his parish church, by the archdeacon and thus given possession of the temporalities of the parish. Together, Institution and Induction assign the spiritual and temporal responsibilities of the Incumbent and are the legal basis of his office.

* * *

Institution

The ceremony at which the diocesan bishop (or his nominee) hands over exclusive responsibility for the 'care of souls' to the newly appointed incumbent, normally in the main church of his parish, at a service attended by parishioners and representative clergy of the Rural Deanery. In their presence, the priest promises to fulfil his duties according to the law and to custom (refer *patronage*).

Insurance

The PCC is obliged by law to insure its buildings including the church against fire. The PCC may exercise discretion to carry more insurance of chattels and other properties.

Lay Participation

Prior to 1921 the administration of a parish fell almost entirely upon the churchwardens, holders of the ancient office to uphold the law within a parish.

With the establishment by the Church Assembly of Parochial Church Councils much responsibility passed to lay members. More recently, lay persons, other than deaconesses and readers, have also increasingly contributed to the conducting of church services. e.g. reading lessons, leading prayers, administering the sacrament at Holy Communion. Lay readers may deputize for absent clergy at Morning or Evening Prayer (omitting the Absolution and Blessing), and distribute the sacrament at Holy Communion conducted by a priest.

Dioceses are developing a variety of Shared Ministry schemes which enable named lay persons to assume a variety of supportive roles within a parish to supplement the work of the clergy, including Non-Stipendiary Ministers.

* * *

Marriage

Marriages are solemnized in licensed places by deacons or priests after *banns* have been called three times in the parishes of the bride and groom and certificates of Banns presented to the officiating clergyman. A marriage service is lawful – that is, it satisfies the civil power, which need not be represented, with the force of a Registry Office ceremony, if conducted according to the Book of Common Prayer, Revised Form Series 1 or The Alternative Service Book 1980 of the Established Church. Marriages may be conducted daily between 8.00 am and 6.00 pm.

It is common for the officiating minister to meet with the couple beforehand to discuss the significance of the marriage service and the details of proceedings.

Fees fixed by the PCC are payable to the clergy and for the use of the church; additional charges are levied if the couple request bells, choir, organ, video/aural recording of parts or whole of the ceremony at the discretion of the PCC and clergy.

Beneficed clergy may conduct a Service of Prayer and Dedication to follow a Civil Marriage; a parish priest may conduct 'second marriages' at his sole discretion after the certification of the publication of banns. A parish priest also has an absolute right to refuse a 'second marriage' service in the church for which he is responsible (a second marriage would be one in which one of the participants has a living former spouse).

Certain clergy known as Surrogates are appointed by the bishop to submit applications for licences for marriage issued by the Chancellor, in cases where the bride or bridegroom has lived in a parish for fifteen days or habitually worshipped there and both swear there is no legal impediment to their marriage.

A special licence may be obtained from the Archbishop of Canterbury in exceptional circumstances permitting lawful marriage at any convenient place or time.

Mattins

Morning Prayer – the long established Christian service said daily by clergy; various forms of service have been approved and published; sermons are not obligatory but are usually included on Sundays and Holy Days. Old Testament lessons, Collects, Epistles and Gospels are listed for Holy Communion: Lessons from the Old and New Testaments are listed for daily use in Morning and Evening Prayer.

Notices

During the church's year various legal notices must be issued – to announce the Annual Meeting and Election of Churchwardens; to announce the Bishop's or Archdeacon's *Visitation* at which he accepts the appointment of Churchwardens and receives their reports. Occasionally, the Vicar will read out an Episcopal letter or an official notice from the General Synod: he has a duty to publish banns of marriage weekly at public services at least three weeks prior to a particular marriage service.

* * *

Parish

A geographic area committed by the bishop to the care of the *incumbent,* commonly called *vicar* or, in some ancient parishes, *rector.* The founder of a parish might have endowed the church building and thus acquired the right to present a clergyman to minister there – i.e. *patronage.* Since 1983 the Pastoral Committee of the diocese recommends the creation or dissolution of parishes and after approval by Order in Council makes the detailed arrangements.

In recent years, some 300 Team Ministries and almost 100 Group Ministries have been formed to cater for changes in the distribution of population and better use of resources.

The Bishop appoints the Team Rector to be responsible for a large or densely populated area either as a freeholder or for a term of years. Together they appoint team vicars who each have the status of an incumbent for a fixed period after consultation with the Parochial Church Council and District Church Councils, if any, elected by the Annual Meeting presided over by the Team Rector. The Team Ministry then functions as a parish probably with the help of other lay or ordained persons.

A Group Ministry is an association of incumbents where each shares with his neighbour(s) to make the best provision for the people in their several parishes; one of them will be designated by election, or appointment by the bishop, chairman of the Chapter and no new incumbent can be appointed without the bishop consulting the other incumbents of the group. Each incumbent has legal authority to assist the incumbents of other benefices in the Group.

There is no connection between an ecclesiastic parish and a civil parish for the purposes of Local Government.

* * *

Parochial Church Council (PCC)

The purpose of a Parochial Church Council is to promote in the parish the whole mission of the Church, pastoral, evangelistic, social and ecumenical, to consider and discuss matters concerning the Church of England or any other matter of religious and public interest, to consult together on matters of general concern and importance to the parish, (refer, The Synodical Government Measure, 1969).

The PCC is the governing body of the parish. PCCs were established under the Church of England Assembly (Powers) Act 1919 and have, to a large extent, absorbed the historic functions exercised jointly by the *incumbent* and *churchwardens*. Their functions have been extended from time to time to meet changing needs and they are responsible for the church buildings and possessions and the forms of worship in the parish and as an 'interested party' must be involved in any proposals for change.

The PCC is elected at the *Annual Church Meeting* held prior to 30 April every year; any communicant over seventeen on the *Electoral Roll* may be elected for a pre-determined period of years. The Council is a 'body corporate with perpetual succession' which means it has an existence apart from the members who compose it; its decisions are therefore of continuing effect. Other members are; the clergy, deaconesses or lay workers licensed to the parish; the churchwardens; the elected members of the Deanery Synod (for three years); at the discretion of the PCC up to 20% of the elected members may be co-opted members for one year; and readers on the Electoral Roll at the discretion of the Annual General Meeting. It is common for one-third of the elected members to retire annually, and the AGM may determine to limit the continuing service of elected members to a specified number of years, e.g. six. The quorum is one-third of the membes and 75% of those present must consent to the transaction of items under 'any other business'.

The PCC shall elect a Standing Committee of the incumbent, churchwardens and at least two other members elected by and from the PCC. The PCC shall meet at least four times during the year. The Chairman shall be the incumbent; a lay person shall be elected vice-chairman; the PCC may appoint a secretary who may be paid and a treasurer who shall be unpaid. If auditors to the Council are not appointed at the AGM the PCC shall appoint auditors who are not Council members, who may be paid. The PCC is responsible for the collection and administration of all monies and financial affairs; the care, maintenance and insurance of the church and of its furniture and ornaments (the churchwardens remain the legal owners of the goods and ornaments and retain their powers and liabilities in respect of care and maintenance of the churchyard), (refer *Visitations*).

Notice of the meeting must be published ten days in advance; notice of agenda must be issued seven days before the meeting.

The PCC may authorize the publication of its minutes.

* * *

Patronage

Patronage is the entitlement to appoint a clergyman to a living (benefice). For centuries patronage was exercised by the patron who had originally provided funds by gift of land or other means from which the parish priest received his stipend; some livings were extremely well endowed in this way. The right of patronage was bought and sold like many other personal assets. Some livings were in the 'gift' of two or more persons who together or by rote would recommend the appointment of a particular priest as incumbent to the bishop.

Sometimes, especially after 1815, the patron was the vicar of the historic parish of which the new parish had been a part. These practices led to great anomalies – a surfeit of parishes in once densely populated areas and a dearth in newly inhabited districts, e.g. in the Industrial North – and to great variations in the incomes of clergy and wealth of parishes, even in neighbouring parishes (refer *finance*). Since 1932, Diocesan Boards of Patronage have sought to reconcile the various needs within their diocese and generally most appointments are now made directly or indirectly by the diocesan bishop. Stipends have been equalized within a diocese (refer *Church Commissioners*).

About 25% of 'livings' in England remain with lay patrons, over 700 with universities and colleges and about 700 with the Crown or named officers of state, e.g. The Lord Chancellor. Almost 4000 'livings' have specific ecclesiastical patrons, including diocesan bishops. An entitlement to patronage can be bequeathed or transferred but not sold and since 1931, except for Crown parishes, the views of the PCC must be considered before the appointment of an incumbent. Under the Patronage Benefices Measure, the PCC prepares a statement of the needs of the parish and two representatives of the PCC should discuss the appointment, which must have the approval of the PCC, with the diocesan bishop.

* * *

Priest

A priest is in the second order of clergy to which men are ordained after at least one year as a deacon and further study and training. Priests are eligible to be 'called to a living'; more correctly these days they are appointed by the bishop (and *patron*) to take charge of a parish. Other priests who may or may not have worked in parishes as priests are employed in cathedrals, schools, universities, hospitals and prisons, or work as missionaries. Ordination endures for a lifetime. A priest may not 'confirm' but has authority to conduct all other services and to give the absolution; he may share with the bishop in the laying on of hands of deacons and priests.

In the twentieth century the Non Stipendiary Ministry has been established. Men and women aged over thirty usually discuss their intention with the Diocesan Director of Ordinands before meeting the bishop's pre-selection panel and after acceptance follow a three year part-time non-residential course of study and training. No formal academic qualifications are necessary. Some financial assistance may be available from the Central Ordination Candidates' Fund. On completion of their course, candidates are ordained deacon: as deacons or priests they have the same authority as stipendiary clergy (refer *deacon: priest*). They serve in the parish in which they worshipped before training but can assist full-time clergy within their rural deanery as appropriate. They are full members of their own PCC.

Provost

The Provost is the senior member of the Cathedral Chapter appointed by the Bishop, in a 'parish church' cathedral, the equivalent of a Dean in an ancient *Cathedral*. He is also charged with responsibility for the Cathedral and its parish, and is chairman of its PCC, which is usually known as the Cathedral Council. He is usually an ex-officio member of the Bishop's Council and takes a leading role in the work of the diocese. He is styled 'The Very Reverend . . . X. . . Y'.

* * *

Reader

Readers are part-time, unpaid lay men or women who after completing a three year training period are licensed and admitted to office by a diocesan bishop who then presents them with a New Testament. The office was revived by Canon Law in 1866. Readers may assist any minister as the bishop considers appropriate and they usually work with an incumbent. They may conduct Morning and Evening Prayer (omitting the Absolution and Blessing), preach, and can conduct funeral services: they can administer the sacrament at Holy Communion but may not consecrate the bread and wine: using consecrated bread and wine stored in the aumbry, they may administer communion to the sick. Most readers also share in teaching, including Sunday School and confirmation classes, bible study discussions and Christian Education generally.

* * *

Rector

An ancient title for the incumbent of a parish who historically received both the greater tithe – corn, hay, wood – and lesser tithe – wool, pigs, eggs. The person or body appropriating the tithes was known as the rector and when he/it appointed a priest who was only allowed the lesser tithe this priest was known as 'Vicar' – serving in the place of the rector. Today, the stipend of the Rector is subject to the diocesan limits. All tithes were commuted into cash payments in 1836. In modern Team Ministries the leader is called rector.

Registrar

The Registrar is the legal adviser to the bishop and clergy and laity on all matters concerning the discharge of their respective offices. He deals with the legal aspects of appointments, acquisition and disposal of land and buildings, the setting up of trusts, common licences to marry when banns have not been called. He attends all *visitations* as the Archdeacon's Registrar. He is always a solicitor and works closely with the *Chancellor*.

* * *

Rural Dean

Experienced clergy may be appointed Rural Dean, to be the bishop's officer within a collection of parishes within an archdeaconry; he may deputize for the archdeacon in specific circumstances, e.g. at an induction but otherwise may be given duties commensurate with his seniority in the diocese – he is usually one of the incumbents in the deanery. One of his roles is to find relief clergy during absences and he is a member of the Diocesan Board of Patronage whenever business affecting his deanery is involved: he frequently may sit on the Diocesan Pastoral Committee. He is ex-officio joint chairman of the Deanery Synod, with an elected lay member. His office is today one of influence rather than power, but when the archdeacon was only the medieval bishop's travelling secretary *[sic]*, his office had greater importance. The role of Rural Dean was revived and defined in 1836. In February 1988, the first woman to become a Rural Dean was appointed in Kent.

* * *

Services

The Canons of the Church of England require that Morning and Evening Prayer be said daily: that Holy Communion be celebrated every Sunday and on major festivals and Ash Wednesday; that a sermon be preached every Sunday; that Morning and Evening Prayer be said or sung in every parish church every Sunday and major festivals.

Stewardship

Stewardship is the name given to a relatively modern endeavour to promote and extend the use of time, talent and resources in the practical application of Christianity.

Schemes enable a parish to budget its expenditure to its income, covenanting schemes enable PCC's to recover basic tax on donations received; 'Collections' is the common name for weekly offerings (alms) made during church services and are the major source of income for a parish – they can be covenanted.

The PCC has responsibility for 'balancing the books'. Each parish publishes a scale of fees for the facilities it provides.

* * *

Synods

Deanery, Diocesan and General Synods were created in 1969 to 'govern' the Church of England. Lay representatives are elected from each parish to the Deanery Synod to serve for three years; and from the Deanery Synod to the Diocesan Synod. Clergy attend Deanery Synods by virtue of their office and elect representatives in equal number with laity to the Diocesan Synod. The Diocesan Synod consists of a house of bishops, a house of clergy and a house of laity, each separately chaired: it is the duty of the Bishop to consult the full meeting of the Synod on matters of general concern and importance to the diocese.

The General Synod, ('the Parliament of the Church of England') also has three houses. It has legislative functions and is also the forum for the discussion of matters of general and public interest; its lay members, representing their dioceses, are elected by ballot by the laity of the Deanery Synods: the clergy of each diocese elect their representatives by ballot.

Deanery Synods discuss matters appertaining to the life and work of the church in the deanery; consider matters raised at the Diocesan Synod especially the raising of the Diocesan Quota (refer *finance*), that is the contribution required from each parish to meet the financial needs of the diocese.

* * *

Vicar

Vicar is the colloquial name for the incumbent of a parish, responsible for the care of souls and public worship. In recent times in lightly populated areas two or more independent parishes are served by the same priest but retain their legal identity. In Group Ministries each incumbent retains his own status; in Team Ministries the senior priest is known as Rector and the others as team vicars.

In some parishes of ancient foundation the incumbent retains the title of Rector.

The Vicar must reside in the parsonage house commonly called the Vicarage.

* * *

Visitations

Visitations are annual formal visits of the Ordinary – i.e. the bishop – or his *archdeacon* at which churchwardens having made a declaration faithfully and diligently to perform their duties are admitted to office; only then can churchwardens assume office. In practice, churchwardens and incumbents of one or more rural deaneries are required to meet the Archdeacon for the visit at an appointed place and due notice of this is given to the parishioners at the principal service on Sunday.

BIBLIOGRAPHY

For further information reference is suggested to the following:

The Church of England in Crisis, Trevor Beeson (Davis-Poynter, 1973)

The Law of the Parish Church, W. Dale (Butterworth, 1975)

The Church of England Observed, Rupert E. Davies (SCM Press, 1984)

A History of the Parish and People Movement, P. J. Jagger (Faith Press, 1978)

The Church in Crisis, C. Moore, A. N. W. Wilson, Gavin Stamp (Hodder & Stoughton, 1981)

Careers in the Church, Judith Paylor (Kogan Page, 1984)

Visiting an Anglican Church, Susan Tomkins (Lutterworth Education, 1981)

A History of the Church of England, 1945-1980, Paul Welsby (OUP, 1984)

How the Church of England Works, Paul Welsby (Church House Publishing, 1985)

Mowbray Parish Handbooks:

A Handbook for Churchwardens and Parochial Church Councillors, Macmorran, Moore, Briden (1986 ed.)

A Handbook of the Ministry, Wilfred Browning (1985)

A Handbook of Parish Work, Michael Hocking (1984 ed.)

A Handbook of Pastoral Work, Michael Hocking (1985 ed.)

A Handbook for Council and Committee Members, Gordon W. Kuhrt (1985)

A Handbook of Parish Finance, Michael Perry and Phyllis Carter (1984 ed.)

A Handbook of Parish Stewardship, Gordon Strutt (1985)

An ABC for the PCC, John Pitchford (1985 ed.)

(Also see list of titles in this Pocket Guide series on page ii)

Reference Books:

A Dictionary of Religious Terms, D. T. Kauffman (Marshall, Morgan & Scott, 1967)

A Dictionary of Ecclesiastical Terms, J. S. Purvis (Nelson, 1962)

The Concise Oxford Dictionary of the Christian Church, ed. Livingstone (OUP, revised 1986)

Everyman Encyclopaedia (Dent)

The Church of England Year Book (Church House Publishing)

Crockford's Clerical Directory (Church House Publishing)

(Also publications of the Church Commissioners, and the various Diocesan Directories)